Another boob of
BATCHES

D1340223

This book contains another selection
of the misprints and absurdities
culled from the press by **Private Eye.**
The majority were sent in by readers,
to whom our thanks are due.

Scores of artistically selected teams of traditional dancers from various parts of Kenya exposed themselves to the world Scouts delegates in a grand performance on Saturday night.

Daily Nation

Another batch of
BOOBS
from
PRIVATE EYE

Illustrations by Larry

Private Eye

Published in Great Britain in April 1979 by
Private Eye Productions Ltd.
34, Greek Street, London W1.

Re-printed September 1979,
January 1980, October 1980, April 1981,
August 1981, December 1982 and August 1983

ISBN 233 97181 5
©Press drain Limited 1979.
Designed by Peter Windett & Associates.

WAKE & PAINE

**FUNERAL DIRECTORS
AND
MONUMENTAL
MASONS**

**31 Church Street
Twickenham**

Phone:
892 3108/1784

*Richmond &
Twickenham Times*

Towngate Theatre
BASILDON 23953

Until Thursday, 7.30 p.m.
Woody Allen : Double film
feature
**EVERYTHING YOU
ALWAYS WANTED TO
KNOW ABOUT SEX** (X)
and BANANAS (X)

*Southend
Evening
Echo*

Two minutes later Edwards scored his first goal for Wales, again from a corner by Thomas. The Maltese goal survivied a battery of shots before the tall blind Chester centre-forward found a gap.

Grauniad

KENWOOD, N6.

Backing on to Golf Course.

6 bedrooms,
3 bathrooms,
3 large
reception rooms,
huge fully-fitted
kitchen.
Central hating.
Armour plated glass
windows.
Double garage.
2/3 **ACRE** garden.
£395,000

Advertisement in Country Life

THE PLIGHT
OF THE LONELY

ALEX is on the way to becoming a down-and-out. His problem is loneliness, and he fears that one day soon it will drive him to a drinking bout from which he will never fully recover.

Alex's story is not unusual — it is happening today, in Scotland's capital city.

Edinburgh Evening News

NEW 40m.p.h. TANK FOR THE ARMY

THE Government yesterday announced a £1,000,000,000 project to build a new 40 mph tank for the British Army.

The plan safeguards 2,000 jobs in Royal Ordnance fartories.

Daily Mirror

Self Pick Potatoes

Available for picking

Friday, Saturday and Sunday
10a.m.-6p.m.
Containers provided.
Phone Hungarton (053 750)
611 for other crop details.
SELF PICK FARMS
South Croxton Road,
Beeby, Nr Leicester.

Leicester Mercury

EDWARDS & HOLMES LTD.

MAKERS OF MISS HOLMES FASHION SHOES AND SCAMPS CASUALS

require

EXPERIENCED

HAND SLASHER

for the Shoe Room

Eastern Evening News

Police found
drunk in
shop window

Kent & Sussex Courier

Photo Sophie BASSOULS (RUSH)

puf

Collection "La politique éclatée"

LES LIVRES DES PUF QUESTIONNENT LE MONDE

⊕ THEATRE LAE

By Popular Request Final Screening Tonight

STAR WARS

Post Courier, Papua

Today's birthdays include: Mr. Robin Day (15); Brig. Sir John Smyth, V.C. (85); the Earl of Cromartie (74); Lord Elwyn-Jones (69); the Marquess of Salisbury (62); the Earl of Gainsborough (55).

Leeds Evening Post

, 7, of Valley Road, Hughenden Valley, near High Wycombe, Bucks, is suffering from a brain tumour and surgeons at a New York hospital have a greed to operate.

Daily Telegraph

Correction

Sir Max Aitken, former chairman of Beaverbrook Newspapers, was incorrectly described as the late Sir Max Aitken yesterday. We apologize for the error.

The Times

HANDEL'S KITCHEN
SHEEP STREET, DEVIZES

This week's Speciality

★ MULES MARINERE ★

Swindon Evening Advertiser

588730   OSP   CELEBRITY HUGHIE GREEN STAR OF OPPURNTUMITY
KNOCKS IS SEEN ,TODAY, ARRIVING AT GULIDFORD CROWN COURT.
THE DISCONSOLATE MR. GREEN IS ACCUSED OF DRINKING WHILE BEING
DRUNK.

LONDON NEWS SERVICE   PIX V.FERIZI   18/7/78   pm

SCHOOL BREAK IN YOUTH TOOK £500 INSTRUMENTS

A youth who stole more than £500 worth of goods from a school was fined £40 at Edinburgh Sheriff Court.

Roy Allan (19), of 61a Woodburn Park, Dalkeith, admitted breaking into Dalkeith High School on January 6 and stealing two language masters, a number of musical instruments, and other items.

Evening News

JUST FANCY THAT

UGANDA DISEASE

President Amin of Uganda in his capacity as his country's Health Minister, has nicknamed venereal disease " good hope " so that sufferers will not be embarrassed when seeing a doctor.—Reuter.

Daily Telegraph

The Chief Constable of Avon and Somerset, Mr Kenneth Steele, provided the first indication that something big was afoot when he was seen at Minehead police station even though he was on holiday.

Crowds of holidaymakers gave the whole affair a carnival back-drop. They gathered around the TV cameras and outside broadcast vans carrying buckets, spades and balloons

Each was charged in turn by Detective Chief Superintendent Michael Challes,

Daily Mail

TELEVISION

RTE

5.05—The Dogon: Concluding the story of an African tribe

5.30—Lorne Greene's Last Of The Wild.

6.00—The Angelus.

6.01—News, followed by News for the dead.

Irish Times

HORSE AND HOUND, July 14, 1978

WANTED

International rider to ride top class Grade A, B & C whores.

Apply immediately to Box H.H 1925.

BIG FELLAH SEND PIDGIN DUKE

The Duke of Gloucester is to talk Pidgin when he formally hands over independence to the Solomon Islands on behalf of the Queen on July 7.

Although the Duke, who leaves today, is unlikely to use such phrases as long long long wisky—to be drunk, and the bik fellah Kwin she like Pidgin chat—Her Majesty the Queen much enjoys Bidgin English, he has been yractising hard to learn the finer points of the argot before the two-weep trip

Daily Telegraph

Actually, nude bathing at seaside resorts is nothing new to this country, or at least certain parts of it, said Mr E. Bareham, editor of British Naturism.

Hemel Hempstead Evening Post

YOUTH WANTED—To train as Petrol Pump Attendant. 5-day week, mon. to Sat., 9—6 p.m. Elderly man would suit. —Marino Motor Works Ltd., Square, Bantry. Tel. 23. 962

Southern Star, Skibbereen

ROY ROGERS

By Our Staff Correspondent in Los Angeles

Roy Rogers, 66, singing cowboy star of many film and television westerns, was in " stable condition " yesterday after undergoing open heart surgery in hospital at Torrance, near Los Angeles.

Daily Telegraph

It does not help that the book is full if misprints and spelling mistakes,

The Spectator

Investment

Sir, — In the first three lines of the last column of my article (October 26) there is a slip which could lead to misshould read : . . . " will depress investment further. Yet in the vestment further. Yet in the long run an increase is essential, etc. — Yours sincerely,
Thomas Balogh.
House of Lords,
London, SW1.

The Grauniad

DRAINAGE DEMONSTRATION

CANCELLED

Unfortunately the drainage demonstration which was to be held at Woodton on May 19th has had to be cancelled due to wet site conditions.

Eastern Evening News

THAT OLD black magic has finally worked its spell on Highgate's own wicked witch David Farrant. He has fallen in love — and he says he's giving up witchcraft for ever.

The girl who has lured Farrant away from midnight rituals in Highgate cemetery is 26-year-old Nancy O'Hoski, a sppepeech therapist from Grimsby.

Hornsey Journal

Mordell Lecture, 1978. Professor J. Tits, of the Collège de France, will deliver the Mordell Lecture at 5 p.m. on Monday, 24 April in the Babbage Lecture Theatre, New Museums Site. The title of the lecture will be *Rigidity*.

Cambridge University Reporter

Paying tribute to his long-standing friend and colleague, Mr Victor Matthews, chairman of Express Newspapers and Trafalgar's managing director, Mr Eric Parker, Mr Broackes said they have done most of the work in building up the group while he received much of the credit.

"So I am glad of this chance to put the record straight, and I am pleased that with the Express in particular Mrs Matthews's personal qualities are getting full recognition ;

Grauniad

The Meat Trades Federation said: "We deplore this approach to any aspect of retail meat sales. Anything which savours of taking advantage of the public is to be deplored.

"It is quite impossible to make a product worthy of being dignified with the name of 'sausage' at that sort of price."

Beef sausages, the law says, have to contain at least 50 per cent. meat, of which 25 per cent must be beer. Pork sausages have to contain at least 65 per cent. meat.

Financial Times

New shocks on electricity bills

Barnet Press

CRAB fishermen yesterday forced the Army to call off a display of big guns as part of its fire power demonstration at the Lulworth range in Dorset.

However, submachine guns and mortars were fired. A claim by a fisherman, Mr Nantes, that a mortar fell in the sea a few hundred yards from his bot was emphatically denied by the Army.

The Daily Telegraph, Wednesday, June 21, 1978

The South bank concert — one of Tjeknavorian's comparatively rare concert appearances in the capital — is a sequence of medieval American chants recounting The Life Of Christ. They will be sung in the original Old American

Music Week

ANIMALS AND BIRDS

BERTIE. Extrovert fawn peke puppy. £150.—Tel. Warningild 412 (p.m.).
RELIABLE, adaptable P.A. overseas sec., exp., 33, domesticated. seeks demanding post.—0376 513640.

The Times

THE Liberals are holding up a Government scheme to extend the exclusive work rights of dockers to areas outside ports and harbours.

Discussions are being held on the measure between Mr Booth and Baroness Seear, the man, in an effort to reach agreement.

Daily Telegraph

Recreation Department

Assistant Cemeteries Superintendent

London Borough of
RICHMOND UPON THAMES

Municipal Journal

Amman press hails stand

Amman, March 3, (AP) — Amman newspapers echoed King Hussein's new hard line t o d a y a n d deplored Egypt for "declaring war on West Australian eggs left to make peace with Israel."

Kuwait Times

The Wilmslow & District Orchestral Society,
Hon. Sec. Mrs. N. Williams,
19 Langham Road,
Bowdon,
Altrincham,
CHESHIRE

Dear Patron or Non-playing Member,

The orchestra will be holding its annual cheese and wind
party on Friday, June 16th at 8.00 pm at the above address.

Sir David listed Mr Bessell
himself; David Holmes, one of
the accused; Sir Frank Soskice
and Mr Reginald Moulding,
former Home Secretaries,

Daily Telegraph

**QUALITY CONTROL
IN PRINGING
Short Course 11-13
October 1978.**

PETER Daisley of Daisley
Associates Limited, con-
sultants in Quality Manage-
ment, is again collaborating
with the London College of
Printing in organising a
Quality Control in Printing
short course.

*Journal and
Graphic Review*

A youth was sent to prison for three months today for
urinating against a fence during Saturdaay's Second Division
soccer match between Brighton and Spurs.

William Hickey, 19, of Kemshot Road, Streatham, London, was
jailed by Hove, Sussex, magistrates

Press Association

THE GREEK ODYSSEY

A holiday in the Greek Islands for £65. Yes, it is possible. £65 jets you Gatwick/Athens return and procures 5 days of abysmal accommodation (£69 2 weeks). Telephone now for brochure and limited availability:

REDWOOD TRAVEL LTD.,

455 Fulham Road,
London S.W. 10.
Tel. 01-351 3169.

A·BTA Member   ATOL 382B

Grauniad

"The Chris Barber Band" (BBC-2, 9.30) are seen in the concert which celebrated Christ's 21st year as a bandleader.

Bristol Evening Post

Mrs Carson's husband, a garage proprietor, died almost two years ago in a road accident at Dornie Bridge.

His condition last night was "satisfactory."

The Press and Journal, Dundee

Lights test aims to spot dyslexia

As he follows lines of print, the normal reader moves his eyes jump, stop to absorb one or eyqes jump, sop to absorb one or more words, then jump again. The fast reader will make shorter stops and fewer jumps, taking in more words more quickly than the slow reader.

Sunday Times

Math inventor

EDWARD Begle, innovator of the "new maths" taught to millions of youngsters, has died from emphysema and California.

Grauniad

GIBSON (Life Baron, U.K.), Richard Patrick Tallentyre Gibson; cr. 1975.

Son of Thornely Carbutt Gibson. B. Feb. 5, 1916; ed. Eton and Magdalen Coll. Oxford; m. July 14, 1945, Elisabeth Dione, d. of Hon. Clive Pearson. London Stock Exchange 1937. Served Middx. Yeo. 1939-46 (N. Africa 1940-41; P.O.W. 1941-43; Spec. Operations exec. 1943-45). Political Intelligence Dept., Foreign Office 1945-46. Westminster Press 1947, Dir. 1948. Dir. of Whitehall Securities Corpn. 1948-60 and 1973. Dir. Financial Times Ltd. 1957, Chrmn. 1975. Dir. Economist 1957. Dir. S. Pearson & Son 1960, Dep. Chrmn. 1969. Chrmn. Pearson Longman 1967. Chrmn. Arts Council of Great Britain 1972-77. Chrmn.-elect National Front. Cross-Bencher. *Address, The Lord Gibson, Penn's Rocks, Groombridge, Sussex. Brooks's and Garrick Clubs.*

Publishers Correction

1978 Edition of
Dod's Parliamentary Companion

Reference to **Lord Gibson's** biography on page 122; for National Front *read* **NATIONAL TRUST.**

SPOTLIGHT

Stale bun reconstituter

Barbecue King's Bifty electric hot jet steamer is a fast, roll or bun heater. A bun is pushed onto needles on top of the machine that instantly pass superheated steam right inside the bun, heating 5 or 6 in a minute. Deep frozen rolls can be heated quickly and stale rolls can be rejuvenated. For more information, please telephone Reading 53447 or quote *CHM 614C* on your Reader Enquiry form on page 55.

The Rt. Hon. Edward Heath, Member of Parliament and former British Prime Minister, will be Keynote Speaker at the 'Diversification of Hong Kong's Industries' Conference to be held on Friday, 26 May 1978 at the Sheraton Hotel.

Mr. Heath will address himself on the topic of 'Shifts in World Trading Partners and their Impacts'.

South China Morning Post

Weather Watch

Copenhagen	12	54	20	68	C
Geneva	17	63	23	73	S
Johannesburg	9	48	22	72	S
Lisbon	16	61	31	88	S
London	12	54	19	66	S
Los Angeles	21	70	30	86	Cl
Madrid	13	55	31	88	S
Manila	24	75	26	79	R
Mexico City	11	52	19	68	C
Montreal	15	59	24	75	Cl
Moscow	13	55	20	68	C
Neasden	12	54	19	66	S
New Delhi	24	75			

Kayhan International (Teheran)

BRONTE COUNTRY.—17th Century luxury cottage. Ideal honeymoon. Sleeps 2/5. Tel. 0282 867540.

The Times

COMPLETE
MEN'S WEAR

PONCE
MEN'S WEAR
UNA CASA MODERNA CON MERCANCIA NUEVA
225 EAST FLAGLER ST., MIAMI, FLA.
AL LADO DEL HOTEL PONCE DE LEON

William Mann picks the early Shostakovich opera, The Nose, "with a virtuoso performance by Eduard Akhimov." (SLS 5088)

Robert Layton was also tempted to pick The Nose, but faced with so many Shostakovich novelties, settled for his song cycles

Soviet Weekly

The former Editor of Punch joins The Express

D WILLIAM ■ avis

Now for the good news...

Daily Express

The hotel selected is the Solazur, the largest in Tangier, which is on the edge of the Bay of Tangier and only 15 miles walk from the bustling town centre.

MAIDENHEAD AMATEUR OPERATIC SOCIETY
(Affiliated to N.O.D.A. and a member of the Southern Arts Association)
Formed 1950

Honorary Life Members:
Mrs. S. Smith   The late Mrs. A. Whitford   J. Wingfield, Esq.

US photographer to do portraits of leaders

Arnold Newman, the American photographer, has been commissioned to take about 30 portraits of leading people in Britain. They will appear in an exhibition, The Great British, at the National Portrait Gallery in the autumn.

His subjects will include Mr James Callaghan, Dr Coggan, Ma Edward Heath, Sir John Betjeman, Lord Goodman, Miss Mary Quant, and Morecambe and Wise. The exhibition is being sponsored by The Sunday Times.

The Times

In a surprise approach, the Somalis overran the mountain peak village of Kombulcha, seven miles north of Harrar, They approached from an almost impregnable angle and pushed down the mountain into the town itself early on Wednesday.

Grauniad

PLEASURE VESSEL FOR SALE

Inboard Engined Motor Cruiser
Colour of Hull — White
Superstructure: Vanished

South China Morning Post

In the courts

Facts hold up case

South China Morning Post

BBC 2

9.0 LIBERAL PARTY BROADCAST.
9.10 ONE MAN AND HIS DOG.

Daily Express

The favours which Pottinger accepted from Poulson throughout the 1960s included four-figure cheques, train tickets, a Hellenic cruise and other family holidays, a car and the run of his teeth at the Dorchester.

Sunday Telegraph

The conference's attitude was indicated by the almost total lack of applause after Mr Wilson's 30-minute speech while Engineering Union leader Bryan Stanley was greeted with sustained crapping when he put the anti-common market case.

Times of Zambia

MP is guest

Sir Edward Brown, MP, attended a coffee morning given by Newbridge Ward Conservatives at 11 Combe and stole £39.

Bath and Wilts Evening Chronicle

Charming blonde JEAN HARRINGTON plays Connie in the BBC 1 hit series "All Creatures Great and Small." Jean formerly played a secretary in "Crossroads," but she's recovered now and is acting again.

Glasgow Evening Times

TWO Crystal Palace footballers pleaded guilty at Inner London Crown Court yesterday to possessing 250 100-dollar American bills knowing them to have been forged.

They were Barry Silkman, 25, of Commercial Street, Stepney, and Rachid Peter Harkouk, 21, of Stamford Brook Avenue, Hammershit.

As they moved up the central aisle past the chair of St Augustine, one was reminded of the erotic titles some of them bear. Here were the bishops of The Arctic, Cariboo, Fond du Lao, Omdurman

Daily Telegraph

P.G. Police Say Detective Shot Man With Knife

Washington Post

THIS IS the fifth Newsread in an initial series of eight aimed at helping those who find it difficult to read.

The column has been written in conjunction with the Oxfordshire Adult Literacy Campaign.

A NEW £250,000 sewage treatment works for Chipping Norton got under way on Monday when County Councillor Oliver Colston performed a brief inaugural ceremony.

OXFORD JOURNAL

Seven months of talks had failed to evolve a compromise and all during May militant threats worried the usually labor peace-loving Swedes. SAF, the Swedish Employers' Confederation, and LO and PTK representing 1.3 million blue and white collar workers failed to reach agreement on a bid presented by a three-man meditation committee.

Sweden Now

Managing director in drink case

MANAGING director Albert Boozer was charged yesterday with driving his Jaguar car when he had had too much to drink.

Mr Boozer, 43, of Rochester Road, Burham, pleaded not guilty at Canterbury Crown Court to driving with excess alcohol in his blood in Gillingham in February last year.

Police on patrol duty saw Boozer's car straddling the white line in Canterbury Street, Gillingham, in the early hours of the morning, the court was told.

The trial continues.

Gravesend Evening Post

YOUNG FARMER With 100 acres would be pleased to hear from young lady with tractor View to friendship, possibly matrimony. Please send photograph of tractor

Evesham Admag

Air India office target of bombs

LOS ANGELES (Reuter) — The Soviet Union has bought more than $2 million worth of U.S. raisins and dried prunes, a California grower says.

The Toronto Star

Mr. Rost: How can British Airways no decisions over the past three years to State for Trade that Ross Stainton be help the industry get any projects launched and now presides over the run-down of the nationalised aerospace industry?

Mr. Kaufman: The hon. Gentleman is characteristically inaccurate.

Self contained living accommodation. Duel purpose Lounge/Bedroom. Separate Kitchen and Bathroom. Ideal two person family accommodation.

From £3,600 Ex Works

Sunday Times

DOG KENNEL, suit medium sized dog. Good condition. Very turdy. Buyer collects £9.99. 19 Beaupre Ave, Outwell, after 6 pm or weekends.   69W

Wisbech Standard

Part-time Job

An unexpected vacancy for a

**KNIFE THROWER'S
ASSISTANT**

Please apply in writing to the:

City Show Office

**Blackhorse Lodge
Great Linford
Milton Keynes**

26-KO-1C

Milton Keynes Gazette

10.35 Fabulous Animals
resented by David Attenborough
6: *Man or Beast*

Radio Times

TWO members of a mountain rescue team earned the thanks of a Llanberis youngsters in trouble on a 3,000-foot woman before setting off to help two Snowdonia ridge.

Liverpool Echo

Some people are being overcharged on funeral costs, the Lord Mayor of Norwich, Mr. Ralph Roe, told the city's health committee yesterday.

"Some people are being taken for a ride by funeral directors," Mr. Roe commented.

Eastern Daily Press

Correction

Last week, we described the new Convenor of the teacher education sector of the London Students' Organisation, Val Furness, as "a Communist Party candidate." She feels this description is ambiguous and needs to be clarified. She is a member of the Communist Party of Britain (Marxist-Leninist). She is not a member of the Communist Party of England (Marxist-Leninist), or the Communist Party of Great Britain, the Communist League, or the Communist Federation of Britain (Marxist-Leninist). She would like to say that she is not in the Broad Left either.

Mr Steel : Appalling picture

Grauniad

Please turn over

Sir,—I write to record my protest at the increasing tendency for sections of an article, to be scattered t h r o u g h o u t the m a g a z i n e. It is extremely
(Please turn to page 46)

N.Z. Listener

Miss Blackwood 1978

First prize £90

PLUS THE CHANCE TO ENTER MISS WALES.

CENTRAL LONDON Socialist Worker meetings on sexual politics. Roebuck pub, Tottenham Court Road, London WC1, on alternate Thursdays at 7pm.

14 October: Lesbians—the double oppression Speaker Sybil Cock.

Socialist Worker

DAVID ATTENBOROUGH — 'sensationally beautiful'

Richmond & Twickenham News

FOOTNOTE: Our Banstead Story series has unfortunately appeared out of sequence. Episode 1y, published last week, is followed by episode 174 this week. Part 15 will appear next week and thereafter part 17 onwards.

Surrey Mirror

Women, Pigs Causes of Wars, Says Commander

The military commander of Irian Jaya and Maluku Vice Admiral Susatyo Marhdi, reiterated that here had been no insurrection in Irian Jaya.

"However, clashes between tribes are common · usually caused by women or pigs", he said.

Indonesian Times

FULL FART

Harold Wilson holder pa a skrive en bok over temaet «å styre et land». Som kjent

NA (Norway)

Newspaper bid?

Trafalgar House, the big property to shipping conglomerate, was last night named as a possible bidder for Beaverorook newspapems. Mr. Bill Keys, chairman of the TUC Print Vommittee said after a meeting at TUC headquarters that the print unions intended to meet all four contenders.

BBC TV's rich tapestry of Britain's Royal Heritage continues tonight (BBC 1, 8.0) with the Tudors, starring (right) the Duke of Edingburgh in the Tower of London with Henry VIII's personal fire-arms, Prince Charles (left) discussing the defeat of the Spanish Armada, and Sir Huw Wheldon, recently magnificently restored through an Arts Council grant, presenting the whole thing. A truly distinguished series.

Vice-chancellors, according to the Association of University Teachers, are paid in the region of £13,000 depending roughly on the size of the university. They also enjoy a range of fringe benefits, notably a horse and use of a university car.

The Times Higher Education Supplement

Best man was the bridegroom's brother, Mr Martin Gasson.

A reception was at Langford's Hotel, Hove and the couple are honeymooning in grease.

Shoreham Herald

Lord Longford
. 'Lord Porn'.

Herald Tribune

Mr. E. Brien

In a report last week of a court case involving Mr. Edward Brien of Scottes Lane, Dagenham, we wrongly stated that Mr. Brien had previosly been found guilty of buggery.

The charge referred to was, in fact, one of burglary

Dagenham Post

Thought For Today

The whle wrod is in a state of chassis.

—Sean O' Casey

The Rising Nepal

2 escape

TWO Fast Germans escaped to West Berlin during the night in the second escape this week, police said yesterday. The two 18 and 19, managed to slip past the border East obstacles without attracting the attention of East German guards. — AFP

Hong Kong Standard

Teutonic Bore excitement

Financial Times

MALE or FEMALE TRAINEE SPONGERS

Number of Young Persons required as Trainee Spongers. This is an opportunity to acquire pottery skills and to work within an expanding company.

Telephone our Personnel Manager for an interview appointment. Telephone S.O.T. 261031.

TAUNTON VALE INDUSTRIES LTD.
NORFOLK STREET, SHELTON

Stoke-on-Trent Evening Sentinel

URGENT. I have spent 2 months looking for a 2 bedroom flat on house at a fair price. Will consider furnished or unfurnished, buying or renting. Greatly prefer Hampstead, Highgate, Maida Vale. I am an hon-rst,ial bglwit heo ,wrpe nrnkiesoe est, reliable, working person with good references.

London Weekly Advertiser

Cllr. JEAN JONES
'"Erotic but
tasteful"

Slough Advertiser

THE LOW standard of literacy and numeracy displayed by so many of to-day's school leavers has become a favourite grouse among employers. They were at it again only last week. Representatives of the engineering, rubber and plastics industries went before a House of Commons committee to complain—for the umpteenth time —about the bad grammar, the poor spelling and the mathematical incompetence of their younger employees.

Financial Times

Girls for boys' school

A school for boys, Sexey's School, Lusty Hill, Bruton, Somerset, is to take 22 girl pupils in September.

The Times

A SPECIAL GUARDIAN
HOME FINDER FEATURE
APPEARS ON PAGE

Grauniad

Generous new county grant for transport

Cambridgeshire is to receive a transport grant of £1 next year . . . considerably more than this year's grant. Commentinting on the announcement last week, deputy county surveyor Mr Alen Tucker said it was almost exactly what they had asked for.

The council now had to decide on their £7 transport budget.

The Hunts Post

Any moves by a reconvened Geneva conference to have British officials installed in key positions in an interim Government would be " MUTTERLY REJECTED," Mr Frost declared.

Grauniad

Opera

The most significant aspect of the year's work by the Welsh National Opera and Drama Company was the first visit of the Company to the new university theatres and the Clwyd Arts Centre. A production of *Albert Herring*, Britten's comic opera, was specially mounted for this purpose and it was presented at the Sherman Theatre, Cardiff, before visiting other theatres in Aberystwyth, Bangor and Mold.

The year saw the momentum lost the previous year (due to financial difficulties) regained with six new productions. Of these, *Jenufa* (Janacek) was the first joint production with Scottish Opera and marked a very suspicious financial and artistic collaboration.

The Arts Council Annual Report

Sailor clings to buoy for 17 hours

Brighton Evening Argus

Last time out the Armagh boys accounted for Castle-blayney and the wide open spaces of Omagh will suit their style of play. It promises toben acentr   fuck it — to be an entertaining game, which could go either way.

Irish News & Belfast Morning News

'RADICALS' TAKE LEAD IN CHINA

By NIGEL WADE
in Peking

CHINESE plovincial leaders are calling for tighter party discipline and stricer public security measures to prevent factional disorder in the post-Mao period.

Daily Telegraph

Derek Sydney Szuilmowski, aged 20, was wearing a skirt, cardigan, underslip, two pairs of tights, panties, and a bra when he sped through Camp Street shortly after midnight, it was stated at Salford.

Manchester Evening News

Raymond Leo Scnultz, 37, of Calumet City, south of Chicago, had a record of arrests which included episodes with the American Nazi Farty, authorities said; and the initials "A.H." may have stood for Adolf Hitler.

Jerusalem Post

A remittance prince? While the British press speculates that **Prince Andrew** is being sent to Lakefield College School to help Canada through a constitutional crisis, our sources tell us that the real reaxon for the prince's being sent to Cannadda in midterm is that heb xng bi& ng $!(((prondi iic456— % BNOThb;t cppty whhhhhhenn e9090 ()() whch isssn't too sprising to those who know the boy's private interests.

Toronto Sun

The XIV School is housed in Druid Stoke House, Druid Stoke Avenue, and currently has a roll of 80 boys between seven and 103 although it does take a few boys from the age of five.

Bristol Evening Post

Manchester Evening News

The general's bequest

MAJOR - GENERAL Henry
Alexander, the controversial
figure at the centre of a war
secrets trial at the Old Bailey
in 1971, has left over £40,000
to the woman he fell on live
two years ago.

Evening Standard

Advertisement in Vogue

245

A blue glazed candlestick holder, modelled in the form of
Kuan Ti (Sod of War) crouching on a rectangular plinth
and holding the sconce and drip pan on his head, his face
left in the biscuit and applied with bearded tufts, his blue
glazed armour with areas also left in the biscuit, 23*cm. high,*
18*th Century*

Phillip's catalogue of Chinese and Japanese Ceramics

After the tour of treasures the dowager Countess of Rosebery relaxes in a seventeenth century chair that once belonged to a Venetian Dog.

Arab World

In the 17th and 18th Centuries, for instance, a reliable guide to the wealth of a country yeoman would be the sort of table he kept and in particular the kind of ware he ate from. If he were very rich he might expect to eat off silver or if he were poor, off unglazed earthenware. Those in the middle used pewter or a glazed and decorated earthenware known as Delft.

Surrey Daily Advertiser

Pepys, by Richard Ollard (Pan Books, £1.50). Not the diary itself, but an account of the man who proved that writing disbars no man from wrenching.

Bournemouth Evening Echo

Births

BAILEY. — On Monday Feb. 14th at St. Davids Hospital to Denise (nee James) and Tony, a git of a són Stephen.

Penarth Times

BUILDING LAD
FOR SALE

Enquiries to:

R. E. GRAHAM & SON
Estate Agents, Valuers & Surveyors
6 CLARENCE STREET
GLOUCESTER. Tel. 21177
Quoting Ref: JG/HS

Chief Inspector Ronald Holdway of the West Midlands Constabulary angered delegates by telling them they did not care enough.

Hundreds of schools did not want to know about crime prevention, he said. They did not put up posters or show films such as the Home Office production *Don's Go With Strangers.*

Times Educational Supplement

Catering College head cooked
for the Queen

Ulster Commentary

Man stole purse at public house

A CHARD man who stole a nurse from the bar of a local public house, admitted the theft when he appeared at Ilminster court last Wednesday.

Alfred John Wallbridge, aged 44, an engineer, of 8A Holyrood Street, Chard, admitted stealing the nurse

Chard & Ilminster News

Couple in car fined

Neighbours complained to the police about the conduct of a couple in a car, magistrates at Whitby heard yesterday.

The couple, Geoffrey Tolhurst, 41, a sales director of Wathside Cottage, Goathland. and Andrea Bell, 28, of Ruswarp Lane, Whitby, were each fined £10 after admitting to insulting behaviour likely to cause a breach of the police at the Wilson Arms car park, Sneaton.

Middlesborough Evening Gazette

KINGSLEY AMIN, the famous British author who won the Somerset Maugham Award.

Rawalpindi Morning Post

9.55 Autumn Ballet created especially for television

10.10 Orson Welles's Arse and

10.10 Sunday Cinema: Orson Welles's Touch of Evil, Charlton Heston, Janet Leigh, Orson Welles

Kent and Sussex Courier

The lists of lust

By Susannah Clapp

Times Literary Supplement

7. Sir James Duncan died on 30th September, 1974 and I take this opportunity of recording, on behalf of the police service, the debt of gratitude owed to Sir James for his thoughtful and generous gesture.

SCOTTISH HOME AND HEALTH DEPARTMENT

St. Mary's, Hitchin

PARISH FESTIVAL CONCERT

Mendelssohn — Hymn of praise

Kodaly — Miss A. Brevis

and works by:

Bach, Soler and Colin Hand

In court—the men in bareback minis

IPOH, Wednesday.

THREE men dressed as women were fined $100 each today when they pleaded guilty to soliciting for immoral purposes in Cockman Street this morn-

New Straits Times, Malaysia

He hopes undertakers would be able to cooperate with a new system, even though it made arrangemtnes more difficult for them.

The Rural Dead of Cowley, the Rev Robert Jeffrey, said he was concerned about the pastoral care given the bereaved.

Oxford Times

Useful Point for Villagers

Thornhill Baptists 1, Braishfield 1

Braishfield's Saturday side had problems in fielding a team for their away match against Thornhill Baptists, and started with ten men. Mick Harfield arrived late and made the eleven, despite the tragic news that his wife had passed away early the same morning. Everybody was stunned to hear this, and at half-time both teams observed two minutes' silence in respect. The idea of Mick playing was to take his mind off the matter and he was a hero indeed to stay for the duration of the match.

The Romsey Advertiser 21/3/75

FIT AND WELL

Mrs. Rosina Harfield asks us to point out that reference to her in the report of the Braishfield football match last week was completely untrue. She is fit and well, and we would like to apologise to her for any upsets the report could have caused.

The Romsey Advertiser 27/3/75

At 3.40 p.m., a member of the TUC catering staff disclosed that the Russians and their hosts had sat down together to a lunch of smoked salmon, roast chien, roast potatoes and a choice of vegetables, fruit salad, cheese and biscuits, coffee and vodka.

Daily Telegraph

Opposition to this came initially from Mr Clive Jenkins, General Secretary of the Association of Scientific, Technical and Managerial Staffs, who said monitoring could not work. He had 9,000 negotiating nits in his union

The Grauniad

A SILVERY June afternoon. A June afternoon in Paris 23 years ago. And I am standing in the courtyard of the Palais Royal scanning its tall windows and wondering which of them belong to the apartment of Colette, the *Grande Mademoiselle* of French letters.

Truman Capote
Daily Telegraph Magazine

Government authorities are still inquiring into allegations of "massive criminality" made by Knowles who admitted 13 charges of corruption and two of conspiracy.

It was stated that he had received brides over a period of four years to "favour" two other companies,

Daily Telegraph

The Malloch International Sporting Agency Ltd.
In Association with
John Birth Sporting Organisation

Directors: J. Birth (Managing)
J. O. Death

Talks about the constitutional means of transferring power to Franco's heir, 37-year-old Prince Juan Carlos, were suspended when the deterioration in the Caudillo's condition became plain. Franco slipped towards death when the supreme poker that ne has exercised for 36 years still clutched between his hands.

The Observer

SAMUELSON.—On Oct. 20, 1975, peacefully, VIVIAN FRANCIS SAMUELSON, M.C. (Poof), aged 90 years, of St Helens, I.o.W., beloved husband of Win and dear father, grandfather and great-grandfather. Cremation private. Family flowers only, but if desired by his own wish donations to Ryde I.o.W. County Hospital. No letters, please.

Daily Telegraph

Man in Thames had a drink problem

'PILE of discarded clothes on the Thames-side promen.

Reading Chronicle

London's new Lord Mayor goes for youth

Premier Carlos Arias Navarro went twice yesterday to Franco's palace, where the chief of state was attended by his wife and daughter and a team of socialists. Between the two trips the Prime Minister conferred with Juan Carlos.

Jerusalem Post

ELSAN TOILET with 1 gall sanitary fluid, used once. slightly damaged, £4.99 or offers. 775 4393 after 6 pm. PAIR SHEEPSKIN LINED Car

Manchester Evening News

APRIL IN
PEMBROKESHIRE
ATLANTIC HOTEL
TENBY FROM £15 DEAD
Any 3 days from 1st April-10

Sunday Times

It's a Kockout starts in April with 21 towns competing for a place in the Jeux Sans Frontieres final which will be held in Belgium in August.

Stage and Television Today

Archbishop Cunnane said that the great friend of the unmarried mother in Ireland, in the past, had been the Catholic Church. It was not possible to relate specific cases, because it was a highly confidential area.

(Photograph: page 6)

Irish Times

11.0
The Korda Season
VIVIEN LEIGH
LAURENCE OLIVIER in
21 Days

Keith Darrant, KC, has just pulled off a brilliant coup in a criminal case. His success accordingly strengthens his chance of becoming a judge.

That night, his brother Larry accompanies Wanda, a mannequin with whom he is in love, to her apartment. There Wanda is met by Walley, her husband from whom she had parted several years previously.

Walley attempts to blackmail Wanda and, in a souffle, Larry accidentally kills him . . . (black and white).

TV Times

NANYUKI farmer seeks lady with tractor with view to companionship and possibly marriage. Send picture of tractor. Littlewood, Box 132, Nanyuki.

East African Standard

THE 35-nation European summit must provide performance not just pledges, President Ford warned on arrival in Helsinki yesterday.

His cautious words were obviously directed at critics in America—particularly in Congress—who think he and Dr Kissinger have given too much ground to humour the Russian in agreeing to sing the 30,000-word Helsinki declarations this week.

Sunday Telegraph

SELFISH MOTIVES
He told Guildford Liberals the best recent news was that a growing number of M.P.s were willing to back a change in the electric system. Opposition was still strong and usually based on the most selfish motives.

Surrey Advertiser

PRESIDENT AMIN
Arrives in Tripoli

PRINCESS ANNE
In Netherlands

Savannah Evening Press

ELEVEN out of the 15 dismissed clerical officers at the Federal Government-owned Agricultural Research and Training Station (FARTS), Umudike Umuahia, have been re-engaged.

Nigerian Daily Times

Page 7

Blonde with gelignite held

Evening Standard

Cats at sea

SIR—Although I can appreciate the reason why cats have been banned from ships, I cannot help feeling that pussy will be greatly missed by all hands on board.

The Daily Telegraph

This photograph effectively shows the thick upper lip and prehensile mouth of the thick-lipped grey mullet.

Angling

LORD Snowdon greeted Princess Margaret as she flew into Heathrow today with a welcoming hiss —

Evening Mail

QUEEN TOASTED BY AMIN

Daily Telegraph

But Coun. Mrs Carol Denham objected. "We may all use some form of family planning, but we don't want it rammed down our throats like this."

Evening Dispatch

GOLDA WINS BY A NOSE

With the unexpected death on February 6 of Qazim Edhem Kastrati, the Albanian community in exile has lost a prominent member.

The Times

The operation to trap the gang began on Friday when a man arrived from Morocco on a car ferry. His car was followed to Prestwick where police ponced.

THE GUARDIAN

7 Wedding Anniversaries

EWART. Once again your regiment, the Light Dragoon Guards, salute you, and on this special day we ask you to remember your privates for the good service given by them over the past 20 years. From Major Bob. - Captain Jacky, Lieut. George. Sergt. Walton, Sergt. McGuirk.

EWART. To Alan and his lady wife. Comes my salute on their wedded life: Twenty years and still going strong, Makes me wonder how it's lasted so long. Here's to the silver and the gold, Brigadier Braith, the leader of the fold.

Dr. Thosteson

'Could the Pill
Cause Hairy Legs?'

WYNBERG
METHODIST CHURCH
CHURCH STREET
9.30 am: Sunday School
(Primary and Beginners Depts only)
10.30 am: Rev J. BORMAN
7.15: Community Singing
7.30 pm: Rev F. G. HITTLER
Carol Service
Social Hour after the Evening Service
A Cordial Welcome to all

(70747)

Cape Town Argus

Both Bishop Muzorewa and Mr Banana have denied any split,

Grauniad

"The Home Office bends over backwards to help every serious sexual offender," Dr Field said.

THE GUARDIAN

By RONALD HASTINGS,
Theatre Correspondent

MAGGIE SMITH has been named stage actress of 1972 by the Variety Club of Great Britain for his performance in the title role of "Young Winston."

DAILY TELEGRAPH

THE new chairman of the South East London Family Planning Association is Mrs Mary Walker, who is expecting a baby in a month's time.

Croydon Advertiser

WI members learn the attractions of suede and leather

Worthing Gazette

PROOF READERS

A large Printing Company in Blantyre, Malawi, requires the services of two fully qualifeid Proof Readers.

Daily Mail

Prince Philip's drive into Sydney was diverted at the last minute when a gelignite-and-nail bomb was found in a garbage can on the route. Another bomb was found at the central railway station. Police, who put an extra guard on the Prince, said, "We are dealing with a madman."

Financial Times

Twenty-two Democratic Congressmen today sent letters to the House Speaker, Mr Carl Albert, and to the chairman of the Democratic National Committee, the newly elected Mr Robert Strauss, asking for support in a campaign opposing the continued bombing. The letter to Mr Albert suggested that the Democratic Party caucus in the House of Representatives should press for an immediate halt to the bombing and the prompt singing of a peace agreement.

THE GRAUNIAD

Jap travel strike over

Japan's biggest transport strike ended early today after government meditation.

Brighton Evening Argus

Certified man appointed as Tory treasurer

£25m. LITTER COST

Litter costs Britain a staggering £25 million and a million man-hours a year to clear up, "a tragic waste of money and valuable manpower," Mr. Eldon Griffiths, Environment Under-Secretary said yesterday.

He blamed people as the real culprits.

Western Morning News

The Orangemen's decision to join the second group is another severe blow to Mr Faulkner. Now he has only a handful of Unionist associations and a swindling band of MPs to support him.

Grauniad

Call for 'Last Tango' sentences

Jail sentences were demanded by the prosecution in Bologna for the producer, director and leading actors of the film "Last Tango in Paris," but judges last night postponed a verdict to June 4.

Although the film was cleared of obscurity charges in a first trial earlier this year, the public prosecutor appealed against the verdict.

Coventry Evening Telegraph

Newbury Weekly News

VIOLENCE —JUDGE HITS OUT

Nottingham Evening Post

CLASSIC Victoria (opp. Stn.). 834 6588
**DON'T GET YOUR KNICKERS
IN A TWIST** (X)
MOST GIRLS WILL (X).

Evening Standard

During evidence of the arrest, PC John Wilkinson said that John Depledge gave him a violent blow in the testicles. They both fell to the ground.

Telegraph & Argus

To finance all these activities, Mr Brezhnev does not need to hide away and misuse odd sums from party funds : a large slice of the whole Soviet national income is freely available, and freely used. The opening of mail and tapping of telephones are taken for granted, as is the concealing of listening devices. Mr Brezhnev's political police are positively obsessive buggers.

Economist

---

time and time again the Scots found space down the left. Hughes was not a great deal more reassuring, his lack of a left foot being apparent.

Sunday Times

German is held over call girls

By PETER SCHMITT in Bonn

Sunday Telegraph

Ill feeling among staff disrupts hospital

The Times

> Scores of artistically selected teams of traditional dancers from various parts of Kenya exposed themselves to the world Scouts delegates in a grand performance on Saturday night.

Daily Nation

HENDON NEWS

COUNCIL DECIDE TO MAKE SAFE DANGER SPOTS

South Wales Evening Post

The church bids you welcome

Dear Guets,

You have decided to spend your holiday here in Zermatt with us. We are pleased to welcome you and wish you all a pleasant holiday. We, as your religious advisers, are ready to offer help in religious questions. The church services offer us the chance to join in united praise of Gold.

Tourist Information

CYCLING

Poles ahead
on home ground

From Geoffrey Nicholson

Krakow, May 16

The Poles returned to their own country on the sixth stage of the Peace Race with everything within their control but the finish. Over the 151 kilometres from Tatrzanska Lomnica to Krakow, they shepherded the rest of the field together so that Ryszard Szurkowski made sure of winning the Kink of the Mountains competition and holding his overall lead in the race.

THE GUARDIAN

Firemen to show to passers by to

Enoch 'ready to split with Tories'

By ARTHUR HAWKEY

POLITICAL excitement was intense today at Westminster and at Tory Party headquarters as it became evident that Mr Enoch Powell was about to launch his most defiant assault ever on the policy of the Party to which he belongs.

The scene of this politically-historic event was the Alma Lodge Hotel in Stockport, where Mr Powell was lunch.

Evening Standard

WILSON APPOINTS MOSES, 85, AS AIDE

The New York Times, 6.1.74

their appliances attract recruits

Crawley Advertiser

Det-Insp. Roy Penrose said in a statement read to the court that a booklet advertising artificial male organs was found by the police at Miss Jones's home in May.

They also found a vibrating device hidden inside a pouffe.

The hearing continues today.

Birmingham Post

Deputy Speaker

Sir Robert Grant-Ferris, 645, Deputy Speaker of the House of Commons, announced today he will not be seeking re-adoption at the next general-election.

He has been Conservative MP for Nantwich, Cheshire, since 1955, and has told his constituency association he thinks they should find a younger man to take his place.

Slough Evening Mail

SINGLE HANDED CHEF

for

Small Luxury Hotel,
Dartmoor National Park

Maximum thirty discriminating guests.

This will suit a young fully qualified chef who wants to earn a reputation or an older qualified chef who wants a less demanding position.

Apply Box No. CHK 6231

VCX24–210

Caterer & Hotelkeeper

Bishop Mahon said 600 parishes, or over a quarter of the total in England and Wales, had recently written in to support the Justice and Peace Commission's campaign for commitment towards the Third World.

"We cannot be self-satisfied about the problems of the Third World; we need to be perpetually reminded of them. This is the point I think Mrs. Williams was making, that we cannot just sit on our assets.

Catholic Herald

Lavatory Seats

64. **Mr. Kenneth Lewis** asked the Secretary of State for the Environment whether he intends to continue the grant to the Institute of Consumer Ergonomics to investigate the suitability of the British lavatory seat ; and what progress has so far been made.

Mr. Kaufman : My Department has commissioned a research project with the institute, which was first begun by the previous administration in June 1972, is well advanced, and should be completed by the end of the year.

MP leaves council

Mr Cyril Smith, Liberal MP for Rochdale, has resigned from Rochdale council because he "has not been pulling his weight", he said in a letter to the council.

The Times

A SUSPECT letter bomb was found today at the West Glamorgan Water Board's Swansea head office. Bomb disposal experts have been called in and should be at the scene in the next few days.

And police were also examining another suspect letter at a city solicitor's office.

The suspected water board arrived in this morning's post.

PRESIDENT TITO

He's just sold his hotel in Peebles and is currently looking around for another business.

Daily Record

POLICE FOUND POT PLANTS WERE CANNABIS

THE BUCKS FREE PRESS, September 28, 1973

Express Staff Reporter

BRITAIN faces an explosion in alcoholism — with the prospect of a million addicts by 1980.

And most of these will be men and women, says a shock report out yester-

---

Ospreys mating

A disabled Belfast Civil Servant mating at the Loch Garten reserve on Speyside, the Royal Society for the Protection of Birds announced yesterday.

Western Morning News

When Israeli Ambassador Josef Tekoah interrupted a lengthy attack on Zionism by Saudi Arabia's Jamil Baroody and accused him of anti-Semitism, Mr. Baroody repeatedly shouted: "Thut up,"

Evening Press (Dublin)

ZAMBIA ENGINEERING AND CONTRACTING COMPANY LIMITED.

P.O. BOX 3059, LUSAKA.

Requires urgently

2 BLUSTERERS

Zambia Daily Mail

On April 14, a group of some 1,500 Cuban mercenaries and counter-revolutionaries supported by the United States and its notorious clock-and dugger arm, CIA, failed completely in an attempted invasion of Cuba at the Bahia de Cochino (Bay of Pigs).

Daily News Dar Es Salaam

Chambermaid had pot

Brighton Evening Argus

LONDON BOROUGH OF HARROW

VOTE for improved health

Join our ANT-SMOKING Clinic

X **Write to the Director of Health Services**
(P.O. Box 25), Hanover House
Lyon Road, Harrow

Harrow Observer

JOHN OGDON, the famous pianist gives a concert on Saturday in the Wigmore Hall at 7.30 p.m. The programme includes works by Ibbs and Tillett and Ogdon himself. (935 2141).

Evening Standard

THE BRITISH Bankers' Association has sent out its own set of guidelies to members suggesting how they should present information about their profits and margins to the Price Commission under the Phase Two counter inflation rules.

Financial Times

Full-Time and Part-Time
Women/Girls Required
CRUMPET DEPT.
Hours: 7.45 a.m.—12.30 p.m.
1.45 p.m.—5.30 p.m.

Cheltenham and District Shopping Week

Immediately before dashing to the airport to fly home the Prime Minister engaged in some personal and highly unorthodox garden party diplomacy. I did not see him at it myself but he is reported to have done some business behind a tree with General Gowon, the Nigerian leader.

Evening Standard

ASIANS
SETTLE
IN WELL

By Our Political Staff

Daily Telegraph

BRITISH RAILWAYS
LONDON MIDLAND REGION

FOR THE USE OF TRAVEL AGENTS STAFF.   From: Divisional Manager,
BULLETIN NO. W.2.   MANCHESTER.

AGENTS BULLETINS.   Agents Bulletin W.2.
D/PA/1   049-2069   16.1.74.

Due to the present paper shortage, with effect from 23rd January, 1974, items appearing on green paper (Special Facilities), will for the time being be printed on red paper.

All concerned please note.

'Hell to pay if vicars were to go on strike'

$74m hashish haul after joint probe

Straits Times

MINERS who received Trotskyist leaflets at a Yorkshire pithead were today advised by their union to burn them.

The leaflets, which propose a miners' strike as a prelude to a general strike, say troops are being trained in Ireland to confront the workers.

"Our picket lines are going to be attacked, and possibly by armoured vehicles," warn the leaflets, distributed at Manverse colliery, near Barnsley.

"We dissociate ourselves completely from the views," said an NUM spokesman. "The leaflets are being distributed at the pithead and we're trying to have them burned. The men who wrote them represent only a tiny majority of our membership."

Brighton Evening Argus

OTHER ENTERTAINMENTS

INFIRMARY OPERATIC SOCIETY

(I.D.O.L.S.)

— MALE —

MEMBERS

URGENTLY REQUIRED

Leicester Mercury

EDWARD HEATH is the most formidable man to lead this country since Churchill had his second stroke.

Ferdinand Mount. *Daily. Mail.*

Request to have fag at half mast refused

The Irish Times

Bryan Hamilton, the Ipswich player, scored the goal, the headed pass being supplied by club colleague Allan Hunter. The 28,000 crows gave the team a moving ovation at the end of the match, evidence of how welcome football is at Windsor Park.

Nottingham Evening Post

FRINGE OF ASHLEY PARK, WALTON
An outstanding, modern detached house, built only 7 years ago, occupying a superb position on the edge of Ashley Park. The interior offers spacious, well planned main line station. The property is in immaculate condition

Surrey Herald

RAY BELLISARIO — the photographer who likes to catch Britain's royal family in off-duty poses has been caught peeing at Princess Anne's new home from bushes in the garden.

Malaysian Sunday Times

Police urge council brothels

By Antony Terry
Munich

A spokesman, Dr Heinrich von Mosch, said yesterday: "This is virgin territory we are entering—no other city has ever proposed such a plan."

Sunday Times

Even the dancing of go-go grisl on such television programmes as Top of the Pops, watched by millions of teenagers each week leaves very little to the imagination," Mr. Lakin added.
oooooo Judge H. C. Beaumont said:

Yorkshire Post

BAILIFFS BOTTOM FAVOURED

Restaurants specialising in Thai food are still fairly thin on the ground and so far only Sateh seems to have been pinched and popularised. A new and (in my opinion) superior Thai place has just opened, **Busabong, 331 Fulham Road, S.W.10 (736 1713).**

The average price of non-barbecued main dishes and combination rice and noodle dishes is 70p. In addition to the regular list there are daily specialities (Thursday, Stewed Dick and Saturday, Nam Prick).

Evening Standard

'Scrap it' winner

A suggestion made to a Wiltshire County Council staff committee that the suggestion scheme should be scrapped has won a £1 award.

Coventry Evening Telegraph

Organs of dead Bill put to MPs

Belfast Newsletter

HEATH AND THORPE: Strange bedfellows. Heath said "yes" –

Yesterday we were the guests of David Hessayon, the author of those slim but extraordinarily useful and beautifully illustrated booklets in the *Be Your Own Gardening Expert* series. They are cheap, brisk, down-to-earth guides on what to do in the garden, particularly on how to recognize pets and eliminate them.

The Times

A PILOT scheme of **not** wrapping gods, unless requested by customers, is being carried out by W. H. Smiths at 37 of their retail shops in England and Wales.

National Newsagent

A spokesman at 10 Downing Street said Mr Wilson was a National Health Service patient and had not received treatment of any sore privately. Mr Wilson, who is 58, was last in hospital when he was 14.

Daily Telegraph

POULTRY

RENT A POLAR BEAR CHEAP, 45p per hour. Eats anything, very fond of children. 5

Dublin Evening Press

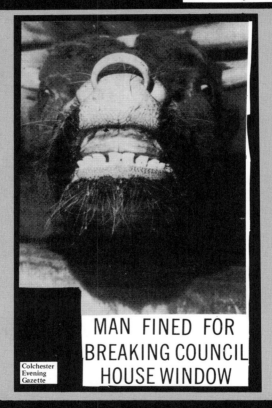

MAN FINED FOR BREAKING COUNCIL HOUSE WINDOW

Colchester Evening Gazette

Committee ; and at the end of the period under review we were delighted to be visited by the Rt. Hon. Sir John Eden, Bt., M.P., Minister of Post and Telecommunications, who with senior Post Office representatives inspected the progress being made on the city's broadcast relay system and the use of the common trench by statutory undertakers.

Milton Keynes Development Corporation Annual Report

THE MIDDLESEX HOSPITAL
Mortimer Street, London, W.1

WANTED—
SPARE RIGHT HAND

THE TIMES

Speaking over the van's public address system, candidate Vanessa Reg Redgrave urged the workers in the market not only to vote for the Party, but to join and campaign for its revolutionary socialist policies.

Spectator

A YOGA Weekend House party
will be held at
SCARBOROUGH COURT
on 4th to 6th August under the leadership of Kenneth Werrel, an experienced teacher who has studied yoga, in Japan and India as well as in this country. Inclusive fee £25. Full details from **Mrs M. Poove, Seaborough Court, Beaminster, Dorset.** Tel : 0308 6262.

Observer

Princess Anne will make a patronising visit

Yorkshire Post

Over the last year, both Mrs Thatcher and Mr Heath have grown in stature. Mr Heath has put pen to paper, escaped assassination, travelled to China, and he is almost as frequent a performer on television as Mr Bert Ford. Whatever might be said of his electoral timing, there is a widespread view in the country that "Ted was tight."

Grauniad

In its fifteenth annual catalogue—Coins of England and the United Kingdom — Seaby's also urges one new design each year of either the 50p or 0p piece to mark some aspect of British industry and invention—preferably related to export.

"We need to blow our own trumpet just a little more vigorously," they add.

Financial Times

the food situation has visibly worsened. Many shops in Luanda have closed·down.

I found only one hotel last night that could serve anything more than soup and fish. The exception, the Tropico, Luanda, was serving guests only.

Daily Telegraph

Mr Ian Macpherson, of Montague Square, was on a morning rum when the explosion happened. "The impact sent things all over the place," he said.

The Scotsman

(8) SHEFFIELD UNITED yehsterday became the first of those teams at the top or the bottom to have their fate settled when they were relegated to the Second Division. United's First Division life, slowly ebbing away since the start of the season, came to a painful end at Tottenham, where they were hammered 5-0 through goals by Willie Young, John Duncan, Steve Perryman (2) and Fartin Chivers.

Sunday Times

★**Turnpike Lane ABC** (888 2519)
CM
To Sat: **'Jaws'** (A)
From Sun: **'Jews'** (A) Bexley-heath for credits.

Time Out

The experiment, carried out by Dr T. H. Rabbitts, involves the introduction of the rabbit genetic material which codes for the production of blood globin into a bacterial plasmid.

The rabbit gene is attached at a particular point in the plasmid's genetic material by the use of biochemical incision,

Grauniad

Mr. Patrick Montague-Smith, editor of Debretts, said today : " I would expect her to carry on as she has done in the past when Lord Snowdon is away.

Evening News

Mr Derek Prescott

IN A report in last week's Times-Advertiser concerning a break-in at the Goat Inn, Codicote, we said that the licensee Mr Derek Prescott had a deaf and blind dog. This is not so, and we wish to apologise to Mr Prescott and his wife Shirley for any embarrassment our report may have caused.

The root problem facing the Foreign Office is whether to treat General Amin's demands as a rather sick poke and ignore them, or to take them seriously, and go some way to meet and soothe his temper.

Daily Telegraph

United goalkeeper, Stepney, went full length to save from Hector and then, in the 18th minute, saved an almost certain goal when he bravely died at the feet of Davies.

The Gloucester Citizen

Later, something like an Algerian-Iranian axis seemed to be emerging. On his arrival, the Sham of Iran said: "The basic and fundamental policy of my country and of Algeria on petroleum strategy are identical."

Financial Times

Spandau secret diaries

By ALBERT SPEER

"Spandau: The secret diaries" will be one of the outstanding books of 1976. Extracts will appear only in *THE HUNDAY TELEGRAPH*.

Sunday Telegraph

Two of those accused of arson and two otters were also tried on charges of disturbing the peace but were cleared on this count too. Two weeks ago

Grauniad

DR. GILBERT, Transport Minister: "One of the greatest social evils of contemporary life."

Financial Times

Martin and Phil Coulter.
Mr. Morritt told Mr. Justice Oliver that the group had lacked experience and advice. "They were told: 'If you don't sign you won't go on Top of the Pope'."

Evening Standard

Shropshire cad

The winning number of the weekly £50,000 Premium Bond prize was 17 ZZ 561284. The owner lives in Shropshire.

Grauniad

Notes. Delete the whole of Note (4) and the operative date and substitute the following:—

(4) Item 1 of the items overriding the exceptions relates to Item 1 of the excepted items; Items 2 and 3 of the items overriding the exceptions relate to Item 2 of the excepted items and Items 4 to 6 of the items overriding the exceptions relate to Item 4 of the excepted items.

VAT News

It was characteristic of Moon that he was ejected from the plane in the Seychelles on the way home—though this was nothing by comparison with earlier exploits which included crashing cars into swimming pools or hotel lobbies or causing havoc at Hollywood parties by dressing

Grauniad

British Rail strike will be total

A SPOKESMAN for the ITGWU said in Dublin last night that the British Rail strike, due to begin today, will terminate all services except those for passengers on foot.

Cork Examiner

Three's company

BARONESS MOURA BUDBERG, who has died in her 80s, brought much style and stimulation to the literary life of London. To the very end, invitations to her parties bore the legend, "8 p.m. to 8 a.m."

Unlike so many other celebrated hostesses, she was as kind to faded old bores as to the shining eminent.

The late Sir Harold Nicolson had a particular place in her affections

Albany: Sunday Telegraph

Friday 24th June

Mid-Glamorgan, South Glamorgan and Gwent (Cardiff-Welsh College of Music and Drama, Thanksgiving Service at Llandaff Cathedral, Civic Lunch ; Caerphilly and Risca).

Tuesday 28th June

Navel Review at Spithead. *Hansard*

Lockheed case witness dies

TOKYO, Thursday. — A Japanese businessman, Mr Taro Fukuda, regarded by Government prosecutors as a major witness in the Lockheed bribery scandal, died in hospital today of a lover disease. He was 59.

---

cash flow. But the employers are expected to pass them on quickly in higher prices, and will be allowed to do so entirely under the terms of the revised Price Cod.

Grauniad

Died

Mar 14. Field Marshal Bernard Montgomery, 88, on Mar 24, possibly of 'euthanasia' as no immediate cause or illness was mentioned.

Impact, Muslim Viewpoints

They were not bored

THE TITLE of a lecture given by William Henry Altor, of New York, at the First Church of Christ Scientist, High Wycombe, was incorrectly given in last week's Free Press as "How to bore and be bored." In fact Mr. Alton spoke on the subject of "How to love and be loved." The Free Press regrets the error which was a misreading of contributed copy.

Bucks Free Press

A £9m. investment to increase cake output has been announced by the National Coal Board. The project will double the size of cake works at Monkston, near Janow, and boost exports.

Yorkshire Evening Post

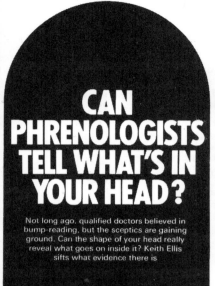

CAN PHRENOLOGISTS TELL WHAT'S IN YOUR HEAD?

Not long ago, qualified doctors believed in bump-reading, but the sceptics are gaining ground. Can the shape of your head really reveal what goes on inside it? Keith Ellis sifts what evidence there is

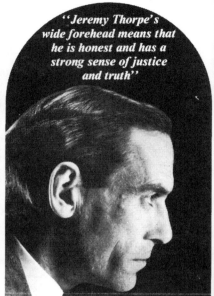

"Jeremy Thorpe's wide forehead means that he is honest and has a strong sense of justice and truth"

Good Housekeeping

Mrs Regina Gray, who runs the Buckland Cat Sanctuary, has six foxes at her home in Buckland. As far as she is concerned a fox will not go for a healthy car.

"In the wilds a fox is much more likely to go for something smaller and easier to catch,

Oxford Mail

L'Officiel Des Spectacles (Paris)

Harlow
Spiritualist Church
Moot House, The Stow.

Owing to the death of

Mr. Chivers we regret we have

to discontinue our Wednesday

Meetings

Thank you all for your support in the past.

Harlow Classified

Best actor: Richard Burton.
Best actress: Bernard Levin.
Best play: Diana Rigg.
Best musical: Sir John Mills.
Best comedy: Brian Rix.

Evening Standard

Students told by judge to leave offices

From Our Correspondent
Manchester

A student sin-in at the offices of Manchester Polytechnic must end by noon on Thursday Mr Justice Arnold ordered in the High Court in Manchester yesterday.

The Times

HOUSE OF LORDS

Die Jovis 3° Februarii 1977

MINUTES OF PROCEEDINGS

PRAYERS — Read by the Lord Bishop of Worcester.

1. Marquessate of Donegall — Report made by the Lord Chancellor that Dermot Richard Claud Marquess of Donegall has established his claim to the Marquessate of Donegall; and ordered to lie on the Table.

About fifty students broke into the college, smashing a pane of glass and chanting: "No cuts, no cuts." A porter had his hand injured. The police

The Times

MAGISTRATES
WERE IMPRESSED

SALISBURY magistrates gave a Bulford man a conditional discharge when he appeared on a theft charge because they were impressed by the way he was trying to help himself.

Southern Evening Echo

More than half the young people who eat meat leave fat on the plate

The Times

We Shoot Children on Wednesdays Without Appointments

DOUG BYRDE
6 ALLISTER CHAMBERS
WINDSOR ROAD.
TEL. NEATH 3310

Neath Guardian

GAS FIRE, Robinson Willey, not used, cost £89, simulated log burning, bargain, £50. Barham Crematorium. Tel.

Adscene

K.S.
FASHION DIARY

IT ALWAYS *seems to be the girls in British Airways whose uniforms are constantly being changed or revamped. So it's good to hear that for the first time for nearly 15 years it's the men's turn. Hornes, the menswear chain, have won the contract and Robert Horne, their chairman, who is also incidentally the holder of the Land Speed Record, is master-minding the new look. If a sneak preview of his initial ideas is anything to go by, the new uniform will, for sheer style in a practical masculine way, make the BA men the envy of other airlines.*

Evening Standard

When is publicity not publicity?

I read Mr Wynne-Morgan's article about creating newsworthy events (October 28). He tells of one of his greatest successes, a hore race in which Angela Rippon took part, to publicise a perfume called "Blazer".

Campaign

Victims of violence in Ulster may get more

The Times

The marriage arranged between Mr Ashley John Badcock and Miss Jane Lavinia Wills-Rust will not take place.

WOULD ANY surviving ancestors of Fred Nerde (Drake's cabin boy) please contact Box 1939 D, The Times.

The Times

Black revolution call

SHOUTS of "whites and Hongkongs (Chinese) go home" echoed through the streets of Port Moresby in Papua, New Guinea, yesterday as crows. spurred by burgeoning nationalism, called for a black revolution and demanded the resignation of Chief Minister Michael Somare's coalition government
—*Reuter*

Sunday Times

GOATS!

On a special occasion, something special counts.

— **A goat for a cake on your wedding day counts.**

— **For a bite during parties, a goat counts.**

— **Enjoy with your family to slaughter a goat on a weekend.**

GET ONE TODAY —

T.S.P.C.A. Building, Morogoro Road, P.O. Box 20639, DAR ES SALAAM Phone 29979/21937.

Dail News, Dar es Salaam

PALACE (437 6834). Mon. to Thur. 8.0 Fri., Sat. 6.0. 8.40
JESUS CHRIST SUPERSTAR
GOOD FRIDAY ONE PERF. 8.0.

The Guardian

SKI.—SAAS FEE, VERBIER. Mixed parties in chalets bang on the slopes. 21st Dec.—Mr. Morrison. 637 4848.

The Times

Lieut. Col. W. W. Manton, and prayers in Welsh and English respetively were offered by the Rev. Gwyndaf Evans, Llandudno, former Archdruid of the National Eisteddfod and the Rev. Robert Roberts. The names of the Fallen of Two World Wars were read out by sex-serviceman Mr. Gordon Hamilton, Llanystumdwy. The Silent Tribute was observed and the Last Post

Cambrian News

In France, truffles are often found by pigs, who have a keen nose for the scent of the underground tuber, although swine tend to eat the plant and must be kept away from the truffles after they are traced.

It Italy, however, farmers prefer to locate truffles with specially trained gods, who can be of any breed and are often a mixed breed.

The Guardian

Triplets... but no surprise

KARIN and Gerald Saltman, of Kevin View, Johannesburg, had .been trying for five years to have a baby—but couldn't.

Then Karin heard of a new fertility drug.

She tried it — and it worked with a bang.

Sunday Express (South Africa)

Meanwhile one policeman manning a diversion sign was not slow to grasp the importance of the situation. He said: "A hole has appeared in the road. Fife police are looking into it."

The Scotsman

FATHER of three John Crowther, who had a sex change operation and lived as a woman, appeared in court at Kidderminster today on charges of driving while disqualified and without insurance.

No ball

The magistrates decided that Crowther should be remanded to the police cells overnight, to appear in court again tomorrow.

Birmingham Mail

Mrs Stonehouse 'delighted'

Mrs Barbara Stonehouse said last night she was "absolutely delighted" that the Prime Minister's Commons statement had cleared her husband's name. It was the best thing that had happened to her family since her husband died — or disappeared — two or three weeks ago, she said.

The Scotsman

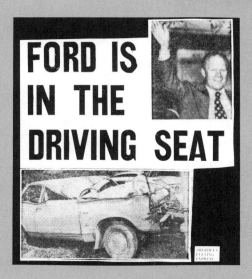

FORD IS IN THE DRIVING SEAT

ABERDEEN EVENING EXPRESS

Transplant man dies

Dusan Vlaco, from Yugoslavia, the second-longest surviving heart transplant patient, has died in Los Angeles. He received the transplant on September 18, 1698.

Belfast Telegraph

Just Fancy That

For those willing to be kept awake, and occasionally hit over the head, "The Bedside Guardian 23" provides top samples of the wit, humour, information, indignation, and sheer humanistic commitment that Guardian readers usually take with their breakfasts. My only adverse criticism is that the book is free of those misprints with which the paper so often entertains us ;

The Guardian

Sir Hugh Cudlipp (above), who writes the introduction to this year's *Bedside Guardian*,

With an introduction by
Hugh Cudlip

The Bedside Guardian

'Homosexuality' could have frightened them off

FEW members attended the November meeting of Gingerbread (an association of one-parent families), and the group leaders wondered if the speaker's subject, "Homosexuality and its effect on family life," might have "scared people off."

The speaker was Mr. Rose Robertson

Harrow Observer

SCORPIO (October 23 to November 22). — A time when it shows how necessary it is for the true Scorpio male to take himself in hand. If this is done correctly there will be a real burst of activity and pleasure.

Lancashire Evening Telegraph

■ Mrs Brett: Took fertility drug

Reading Evening Post

Miss Linda Ann Male, of 29 Blake Road, bicester, was married to Mr Robert Albert Page, of Stock, Essex.

The bride, an animal with Oxford University, is

Oxford Times

EUROPEAN COMMUNITY
(ARCHITECTS)

11.0 p.m.

The Minister for Housing and Construction (Mr. Reginald Freeson) : I beg to move,

Tonight we are concerned with a daft EEC directive on the mutual recognition of architects' qualifications.

Hansard

OWEN. Phyllis. Six sad years today. Don't ask me if I miss you. No one knows the pain. It's lovely here without you dear, life has never been the same. God bless you dear. Loving husband Frank.

Bristol Evening Post

Just four months old

Peter Hall, Director of the new National Theatre.

Lord Wigg, of Warwick Square, Belgravia, London, said nothing during the brief hearing, in which he sat in the wrought iron-surrounded cock.

Evening Herald

In 1908, she joined the Gaiety Theatre, and married director Lewis Casson—a union that lasted 60 years, producing four children and countless performances.

Newsweek

Pay increases in Guernsey

ABOUT 900 civil servants in Guernsey will receive salary increases ranging from £6 to £16 a week from August 1.

The increases, based on the local cost of loving, will add £500,000 to the island Government's present pay bill of £9m. for 4,000 employees.

Financial Times

Granada

10	00	Waterwise.
10	20	Keep Britain Slim.
10	50	Animated Classics.
11	35	Untamed World.
12	00	Rupert Bear.
12	10	Hickory House.
12	30	Three Little Words.
1	00	First Report.
1	20	This is Your Right.
1	30	Crown Court.
2	00	Good Afternoon.
2	30	Racing from Redcar.
4	25	Michael Bentine.
4	50	Hogg's Back.
5	15	Take Kerr.
5	20	Crossroads.
5	50	News.
6	00	Granada Reports.
6	30	Adventurer.
7	00	Don't Ask Me.
7	30	Coronation Street.
8	00	Summer Night Out.
9	00	Rich Man, Poor Man.
10	00	News.
10	30	Rich Man, Poof Man (cont).

Grauniad

time. A half hundredweight would be nearer—and I thinl this is probably high.—Yours faithfukky,

P. Reynolds.

Ipswich.

Grauniad

2.0 You and Me

Shapes and Sizes . . . Balls with NEIL FITZWILIAM and PETER LORENZELLI

Producer BARBARA PARKER
(*Next programme: Thursday*)

Radio Times

Archbishop Sin named cardinal

Bulletin Today
Manila

The police arrested two IRA leaders, David O'Connell and Joe O'Neill, after an IRA funeral later today, but that appeared to be connected to a souffle during the funeral.

International Herald Tribune

Man dies in head-on crash

A MAN died and a women was seriously injured in a road accident near Byer Moor Farm, Rowlands Gill last night.

Firemen using cutting equipment fought for nearly an hour to free the trapped man whose car was involved in a head-on collision with a goods wagon.

He had a surprise in the final stages when members of his family and friends arrived to help out with sandwiches and drinks.

Jimmy, a widower, said: "I'm tired, but I enjoyed it. I might have another go when I'm 70."

Northern Echo

AT-**TENT**-ION

Special heatwave offer

A FREE FAMILY WITH EVERY TENT SOLD

Cambridge Evening News

Orange Lodge praised by LP

Lord Provost Peter McCann last night congratulated members of the Orange Order for the work their movement does to help disable people.

Glasgow Evening Times

Anti-lions Bill

Lions on the lawn, bears in the basement or tigers on the terrace are likely to become rarities under a private member's Bill given an unopposed second reading in the Mouse of Lords yesterday. It bans the keeping of dangerous wild animals as pets without a licence.

Western Mail

"Work of a solicitor," talk by Mr R. Borer. Wendover Mothers' Club, Library room, Wendover, 7.45 pm.

Bucks Advertiser

APPOINTMENT OF

FIRST HEADMASTER

THE INGLISH SCHOOL—ESTEPONA

An Educational Cooperative and Trust (approved by the Spanish Government)

Estepona (Malaga), Spain

Times Educational Supplement

Le Président M. Anouar El Sadate a reçu, hier, M Wright Fogg, Rédacteur en Chef du «Times».

BLIND BABIES COMPETITION

The Mid - Sussex Dart League announce that the finals of their 1971 Blind Babies Competition are to be held at the British Legion Club, West Hoathly, on Friday,

The Mid-Sussex Times

How Heath at 60 sees his future

GLASGOW HERALD Monday July 5 1976

● Would any readers be willing to let me have details of personal fears and anxieties in connection with a book I am preparing on the subject?—(Miss) **S. T. Harris,** 85 Holmefield Court, Belsize Grove, NW3.

Jewish Chronicle

Saws stolen

Two chainsaws were stolen from Enfield Crematorium during the Christmas holiday.

Enfield Gazette

BOGNOR LADIES THRASH PENGUINS

BOGNOR 11 PENGUINS 0

Bognor Regis Post

Female, early forties, wishes to share her pleasure in gardening, music and lively discussions, with a well-educated male who is tall, has a sense of humor and appreciates a keen wind and a warm smile. Object matrimony. Box 273, this paper.

Vancouver Sun

Queen Elizabeth's entourage will include Prince Philips, the Prime Minister and Mrs. Heath

Djkarta Observer

THE WEE SHOP, 3 Main St., Overseal: Glen twin toilet rolls 13½p. Yeoman potatoes 1lb

Burton (Ashby & S. Derbys,) Trader

Brief details regarding conditions of service are set out in the attached copy letter headed "Walk Tall with the City of London Special Constabulary". Members of the staff who are interested should either call, write or telephone giving details of age, height and occupation to:-

Mr K Short,
City of London Special Constabulary

NEWS IN BRIEF

DR CONNIE Mulder, once a leading contender for the premiership0of South Africa, was expelled from the ruling National Party yesterday after refusing to accept the reports of a judicial commission of inquiry into the Department of Information scandal. **Page 6.**

Grauniad

Rape charge is expected

A man expected to be charged with raping a young married woman in Limerick during the weekend, was still in hospital last night — recovering from exhaustion.

Irish Independent

A MAN who "went berserk" after being told that he was banned from a pub caused damage estimated at £1,000.

Robert White (41) threw his glass at bottles behind the bar. When the landlord went to calm the police, White damaged bar fittings,

Coventry Evening Telegraph

Dapper eloquent Mr. Thorpe strenuously denies charges that, with three other accused men, he plotted the murder of Normal Scott, who claims that he and the politician were once homosexual lovers.

Athens News

CHAS. H. BOND
LIMITED
NON-FEROCIOUS
METAL MERCHANTS

Parish Magazine: Duddeston

Doctors urged 'Let Reggie die'

WHEN TV news-reader Reggie Bosanquet was born, his father told doctors: "Don't let him live."

Weekend

Mariners Whip Princess Anne

Daily Press, Newport News, Va.

De izquierda a derecha: Igor Gorin, Sophie Fucker Powell, Robert Taylor, Judy Garland y Buddy Eb: completo.

BUS MOANS: MP TO SEE FOR HIMSELF

Leamington Spa Courier

By Wednesday, it emerged that Mrs Thatcher would not be going on television to take part in a face-to-face debate with Mr Callaghan. Normally, the Prime Minister is the one who turns down such invitations but this time he grasped on the idea fast, believing that he could screw well off Mrs Thatcher.

Irish Times

Perched 20ft above the ground on a narrow ledge Albert, a 15-month-old mongrel, got stuck and had to be rescued by Colchester firemen.

The dog, which belongs to the family of Christopher Blaxill, is the chairman of local firm Kent Blaxill builders and decorators' merchants,

Colchester Evening Gazette

More women required

The Civil Service says it is making "strenuous efforts to improve the quantity and quality" of women

Grauniad